73

PRAISE FOR HER WHOLE BRIGHT LIFE

Courtney LeBlanc writes the way a miner mines for gold—hacking
away at the mundanities of life—each poem striking the treasure beneath
the dark monotony. This book will teach its readers to always look
for the poem in everything, which is to say, it will color your world,
convince you of the unequivocal worth of each unpromised moment.
An incredibly brave collection, this book doesn't lie. It isn't a mortician.
It's real, honest in a way that will force us each to be more honest with
ourselves. When you are jaded by the world, pick up this book. It will
rekindle your love of poetry, of living.

~ Megan Falley, author of Drive Here and Devastate Me

★★★

In Her Whole Bright Life, Courtney LeBlanc offers an incomplete list of
truths: We are all of us small. Running is an escape from crying. Talking
to our beloved dead is basically talking to ourselves. This book reminds
us of the importance of "trying to write about joy," even in the darkest
times, and that "the other side of grief is love." I recognize myself in these
poems—in the anxiety I always feel that spiked during the pandemic. In
the complicated relationship with a mother. In watching a father die. In
trying to find "some heaven / I don't believe in." LeBlanc is the brightest
and bravest poet I know.

~ Melissa Fite Johnson, author of Green

★★★

Courtney LeBlanc's collection Her Whole Bright Life lives up to its title:
it is personal, vibrant, and alive. Reckoning with personal grief for a father
and societal grief and anxiety in the age of COVID, these poems fearlessly
scrutinize the political meaning of personal choices, from the best choice
of movie after losing a parent (Dirty Dancing, of course) to the daily
struggle of disordered eating.

LeBlanc's poems pull no punches; the opening piece, "Self-Portrait," reveals the speaker's self-lacerating internal voice: "I cannot / stop / thinking my body would be better / if there were less / of it." Through lyric reflections, prose poems, and elegies, Her Whole Bright Life obsessively asks what it means to care for a body as it lives and dies: "this is what we do for death, / we feed the living."

The obsessive attention to the dying body of the speaker's father sits uncomfortably close to the speaker's obsessive attention to her own body, barely recovered from an eating disorder ("When I gave up that slow march toward a hungry / death I thought I'd be normal"). The stakes are high here: poetry becomes nourishment, as in 'Prompt,' which lists writing prompts that culminate in an act of consumption that is nearly sacramental, a poem baked "inside a loaf of bread, your mother's recipe [...] With each bite you swallow, forgive yourself."

Through her wit, sorrow, and rage, LeBlanc creates a poetic world that tries to make sense of global anxiety and personal suffering. In these frank, sensual poems, the living and the dead share meals, allowing themselves to be consumed by each other—after all, that's what grief is.

~ Laura Passin, author of Borrowing Your Body

★★★

LeBlanc writes from a place of grief, of memory, and of a fierce love for her father, our country, and her body. What she shows us, with taut tension and evocative language, is that even though we must say goodbye to things we love, there are always pieces that remain with us, constant and cleaving. LeBlanc is such a fierce writer that she makes it look easy and I thank her for this transformative collection.

~ Barbara Costas-Biggs, author of Broken On the Wheel

★★★

Courtney LeBlanc's poetry is piercing, raw, and honest. It dares us to witness vulnerability transforming into power and beauty.

~ Shuly Xóchitl Cawood, author of Trouble Can Be So Beautiful at the Beginning, Adrienne Bond Award winner

Her Whole Bright Life

CB

by Courtney LeBlanc

WRITEBLOODY
QUALITY AMERICAN BOOKS

Write Bloody Publishing

writebloody.com

First edition.
ISBN: 978-1949342482

Cover Design by Derrick C. Brown
Interior Layout by Nikki Steele
Edited by Anna Binkovitz
Proofread by Wess Jolly Mongo
Author Photo by Tay Lauren Photography

Type set in Bergamo.

Printed in the USA

Write Bloody Publishing
Los Angeles, CA

Support Independent Presses
writebloody.com

For my dad: catch you down the road

HER WHOLE BRIGHT LIFE

HER WHOLE BRIGHT LIFE

I.

II.

III.

I.

SELF-PORTRAIT

I cannot stop
collecting recipes, an unexpected
replica of my mother / counting
     calories   seeing
every   bite   an act
I need to   undo / loving
cherry blossoms that rain down
each spring, a torrent of pink petals
falling / or burying
my nose in the lilacs that rim
my neighbor's fence / I cannot
    stop
thinking my body would be   better
if there were less
       of it
I   cannot talk
politics without getting angry / cannot
do a crossword or win Scrabble
    despite   my extensive
vocabulary / cannot keep
   a houseplant alive
I   can
cook and bake and tell you the exact
calories in a brownie / a carrot / my morning
soy latte / can run ten
           hike twenty
          walk thirty
miles / can spend the day
with a book and never
be bored / I can tell you I love
    my dogs more
than anything else / I can
   no longer   survive
on little sleep but also   can no longer
sleep in / I can tell you
who I am but not
    who I want to be

I Don't Understand Black Holes No Matter How Many Times Cody Explains Them to Me

Because the idea that a place is so dense nothing escapes—not light, not sound—is something I can't wrap my small human mind around. *Imagine approaching it,* Cody says, not giving up on my inability to grasp the concept, *but as you enter it you begin to stretch, like silly putty. And even though you'd already be dead because nothing can live in the dark void of space, imagine if you were alive, you'd just keep stretching, infinitely pulled in opposite directions but never breaking apart because the gravity is so dense, nothing can escape.* Some things are just too big for me to understand. Now scientists say they've found a new one, the closest one to Earth ever discovered. It's still 1,500 lightyears away which is another concept I don't understand but that's too much for one poem. For now I'll just accept that black holes exist, that they are closer than we previously thought, and that they are a force so powerful, every mistake I ever made would be swallowed by them.

LIGHT AS A FEATHER

Sometimes if I lie
just right in bed, arms
at my sides, feet relaxed,
the perfect corpse
pose, and I empty
my mind, think only
of a sky, clear after
an afternoon thunderstorm,
I can feel my body lift
from the bed, levitating
in the dark air.

At childhood sleepovers
my friends and I played
*light as a feather, stiff
as a board*—I was a favorite,
my bird body just breath
and skin. My friends'
fingertips slipped beneath
me and I rose into the air,
body held aloft by their small
hands and my sheer will
to be lighter, lighter
than anyone else.

Now I sometimes lie in bed
and will my body to rise,
to be weightless and free,
to feel like I did more
than thirty years ago: proud
of the easy way my body
floated into the air, light enough
to be held up with a chant
and the breath of four small girls.

YOU AIN'T SHIT

You ain't shit North Dakota—you're all snow and flat and forever
horizon. You fly-over state. You MAGA hat, Fox News junkie.
The year I left it snowed on June 1st. June 1st you motherfucker.
Can't bury the dead in a North Dakota winter unless you bonfire first.
My 18th birthday brought a blizzard that shut down a state that knows
how to deal with snow. North Dakota laughed at chains on tires, laughed
at the fools who tried to leave their neighborhoods. My father cleared
the driveway with the snowblower and North Dakota punked him
and dropped another eight inches. As if his work was ever done.
And now, he's dying. You did this to him North Dakota, you broke
him. His whole life spent nurturing you, feeding the world with
the wheat he grew in your rich soil. He never touched the black
tar of long-dead dinosaurs that sits beneath you, never mind the millions
it could bring. And what do you do? You give him thunder-snow.
You withhold the northern lights that have, on rare occasion, pirouetted
across the sky like a bright green ballerina. I saw them once, had to pull
over to gape. But my father has never seen them and now his eyesight
is failing. His hands shake. He's always cold. His one functioning kidney
is stuttering to a stop. It'll drag all the other organs down with it. It won't
take long and his doctor has promised she'll make it painless. If he dies
this winter I'll cut down every tree in every forest across you, North
Dakota. I'll build a fire big enough to see from space. Let the astronauts
think it's the northern lights. Let everyone think the world is ending.
Because for me, part of it will.

FOR MY FRIENDS, IN RESPONSE TO A QUESTION

~ *after Safia Elhillo*

I'm mostly okay which is mostly the truth.
My dad is dying, my dog is needy, my husband
hates his job. I wake before the alarm can call
me out of my dreams (if I dream anymore, I can't
be sure), lift weights, do burpees and crunches.
I bake and sauté and Zoom call. I hike as many
hours as I can spare, always with my dog, her panting
the only noise on the empty trails. I write and read
and edit. I buy $200 in postcards and mail them
the next day. I to-do list and I home-manicure.
I consider the dangers of air travel, my father's
weakened immunity, his only kidney slowly stuttering
to a stop. I stretch and yoga and run. I cry, I sleep,
I hope to touch him in my dreams. I text and I email
and I wait for the sun to set each night, for the watercolors
to splash across the sky, for it to cool enough so I can
sit in my backyard, my dog stalking squirrels, the rocking
of my chair soothing me. I'm okay, I say, after hanging
up the phone, after my father tells me he won't do
dialysis. I'm mostly okay, which is mostly the truth.

WE'RE ALL ANIMALS

A monarch butterfly lands on the marigolds
I've planted, its wings the same fiery orange
as the flowers. It alights briefly on the gathered
petals before fluttering away, too quick
for a camera to capture it, barely long enough
for my eyes to register.

Driving to work I see the remains
of a raccoon, only recognizing
its masked face, the rest of the body
a small mess of fur and bone. I don't want
to look but I always do, my eyes drawn
to the carnage of everyday life.

My dog has a high prey drive—she chases
bunnies, trees squirrels. One evening
a squirrel runs across our fence
and she spends the next thirty minutes
patrolling the perimeter, seeking
the offending creature.

She would likely kill anything she caught,
would clamp down with teeth
descended from wolves, would shake
the animal, the muscles taut in her neck.

She catches a pale blue butterfly. I pry
open her jaw, lift out the delicate
creature. It lies unmoving
in my hand as my dog whines. I toss
it over the fence, onto the lilac bush
that blooms each spring and fills the air
with its heavy scent. The next day I find
it lying on the ground. My dog is no longer
interested and I can only weep.

MENAGERIE

This is the year I acquire anxiety, that donkey kicking
at my chest, my brick heart thumping in response,
leaves me bruised and achy and still unable to sleep.
There's a gerbil in my brain, running marathons
on that squeaky wheel, each lap whispering a new worry
for me to chew on: *Who will die next? When will I find
a new job? When will I be happy?* As if happiness is possible
during a pandemic. As if the weight of living weren't
crushing. Bees bumble around me, ready to drink
my tears, ready to pollinate the world with anxiety.
Think of the beautiful flowers that would bloom—
spiky and dangerous—but their bright colors
would call to the tender flesh of your fingertips, blind
to the thorns that desire the iron taste of blood.
There's the ostrich, its dumb head buried
in the sand, trying to hide from the latest headline.
The gazelle that resides in my nervous system, alert
to dangers real and imagined—is that a bug
bite or cancer? Cough or COVID? WebMD says
I'm likely dying. The cheetahs that hide in my feet,
carry me miles each morning but I still can't outrun
this panic that smolders inside of me. And what happens
the day I smell smoke, the nervous fires stoked for so long
they suddenly rage out of control? The animals inside me
run, trample the tender flowers that sprouted around
my battered heart, stampede for the exit, but find it locked.

WE FEED THE LIVING

The week my father died I dug
through the freezer and pantry
in my parents' house, pulled out
the ingredients to make my sister's
favorite dessert. As I stirred and baked
I thought of my father, his body small
but his hands swollen with edema.
As the peanut butter cookies cooled
on the counter, the sweet smell filling
the house, I stared out the window
at the garden my father planted months
ago. The day before my sister and I tore
it up, the plants done with their offerings.
I tossed the rotten tomatoes and overgrown
cucumbers into the trees for the birds
to find. When we brought my father home
the house was filled with food from friends
and neighbors—this is what we do for death,
we feed the living. After my father took
his last breath we pulled the sheet tight
around him, a pale-yellow cotton shroud.
Then we sat in the kitchen, mindlessly eating
the food that covered every surface, our bellies
filling with grief and the angel food cake
I baked the day before—my father's favorite.

THE NIGHT MY FATHER DIED WE MADE MY BROTHER-IN-LAW WATCH DIRTY DANCING

Because the whole week was exhausting. None of us slept. Our eyes swollen from crying. My throat was so sore I worried it was strep. When the strep test came back negative, I worried it was COVID. The hospital bed still sat in the corner with medical supplies stacked beside it. The neighbors kept bringing over food and so we grief-ate. That morning I woke at 3:45am to give my dad his dose of morphine. I found my mom asleep in the recliner and when I woke her, she said, *I couldn't hear him breathing from the bedroom*. I sent her to bed, tucked the syringe into my dad's cheek and pushed the plunger slowly, the morphine absorbing because he could no longer swallow. I stayed up till 5am, dozed till 6:30am when my mom woke and took over so I could go for a run. Because it's hard to cry while running. And when my dad's brothers and sister arrived I greeted them in the driveway, the day cruelly bright and beautiful. It took his brothers three tries to make it into the house, three tries to say goodbye. My aunt called my sister by the wrong name but none of us corrected her. And then my dad's best friend showed up. It took him thirty minutes and four cigarettes to gain the courage to hold his hand. And when my dad took his last breath, we didn't realize for a moment he was gone. But no inhale followed. And I couldn't find a pulse. I kept my fingers on his wrist hoping to feel the tiny blip. But it didn't come. And so that night my sister and mother and I watched a movie we'd seen a dozen times. We sang along to the soundtrack and laughed when Jim didn't know the plot. We needed nostalgia and distraction and a happy ending. We needed Baby upon that stage, her whole bright life ahead of her.

WHEN MY THERAPIST ASKS HOW I'M DOING

I talk about the election, my father's death, my friend's
brain tumor. I don't tell her about my two and a half
hour workout that morning, how I wouldn't stop until
I burned 1,000 calories. I don't tell her of my daily
ritual of stripping down, exhaling every ounce of breath
before stepping onto the scale. How if I have a hair tie
around my wrist it must be removed and the ritual
repeated. I don't tell her I know the calories of my
morning coffee (102) or my yogurt and granola (170)
or how I fear growing into my mother's body.
I spent a decade eating nothing more than an apple
and two rice cakes between the hours of 8 and 4.
When I gave up that slow march toward a hungry
death I thought I'd be normal. But what is normal
if not tracking every bite of broccoli? If not knowing
the calories in a single baby carrot (4). I don't tell
my therapist this because I like when my clavicles arch
out from my chest, when my hip bones jut forward
like handlebars. I don't tell her because I don't
want to talk about what ended fifteen years ago,
even if its fingerprints remain etched permanently
on me. Instead, I talk about the daily hikes with my dog,
my friend's chemo regimen, the new meditation app
I downloaded. The session ends and I scoop up the
rumpled Kleenex and drop them in the garbage. There's
a bowl of leftover Halloween candy near the exit. I dig
for a Snickers, pop the bite-size chocolate into my mouth
and make it last until I reach my car. This time I don't
record it. This time, I regret not taking two.

SMALL

But even if the world is half bad, it remains / half good.
~ from To The Tender by Kristen Tracy

At 2am my dog paws the side of the bed, telling
me she needs to go out. Blurry-eyed we walk
the quiet streets so she can find the perfect spot—
the world is her toilet, but she has her preferences.
We're having a warm spell and though I know
I should hate climate change I love a 68° day
in December. Scientists say the summer ice
in the Arctic Ocean will disappear by 2035
and this will be detrimental to the animals
that depend on it, but in this hour I am only
grateful to not be trudging through the darkness
and cold. When my dog stops suddenly and stares
behind us, a low growl rumbling past her teeth,
my overreactive imagination thinks, *Serial*
killer! That creepy clown! The blood-soaked twins
at the end of the hallway! Instead, I see
a fox standing in the street, a rabbit clutched
in its jaws. I tug my dog and we keep
moving as the fox watches us, its flame-
colored fur bright under the streetlights.
I forget sometimes how small foxes are.
I forget sometimes how small we all are.

I Don't Eat After 8pm

I once read you shouldn't
eat after 8pm if you want to lose
weight and I, a woman who hated
her body for a decade, always wanted
less to hate. The week my dad died
I ate my mother's pretzel dessert
with a spoon, the pan held beneath
my chin like a trough, the salty-sweet
combination filling my belly with
calories I couldn't begin to count.
I ran seven miles each morning,
the flat stretching before me unbroken.
My father lay quiet, first in the hospital, then
in the living room, no longer consuming
anything, his small frame dark against
the pale sheet. When I came inside,
sweat slick and panting, I kissed his
face, told him about my run, the flowers
blooming in the ditch, the blue sheet
of sky. That night, after my mother
had finally gone to bed, I sat
on the chair I'd pulled to my father's
bedside, ate a cloud of carbs,
the homemade bread my mother
baked and I grew up on. I slathered
on a layer of butter, licked the melted
gold from my fingertips, told him,
in between bites, that I loved him.

TENDER MUSCLE

I see it while driving, a deer on the losing end
of its dash across the pavement. I wonder if its body
bounced, if its lips kissed concrete, if it locked eyes
with the panicked driver before its body slid over
the hood and onto the side of the road where
I spotted it days later. I drive past it for a week,
each time its fur falling away more, each time
its bones more exposed to the winter air. Even
in the cold it decomposes quickly, and soon its ribs
jut upward, reaching skyward toward some heaven
I don't believe in. Still, every time I pass it, I whisper
a word of hope, of prayer, of salvation. I'm moving
too fast to see but I wonder if its heart remains,
enclosed in its cage of bones, if the vultures have
found it yet, eaten the tender muscle.

It's a Lot

~ after Jon Sands

It's a lot to wake each day and lift your body
from the warm bed into the cold morning air.
And it's a lot to then dress for your morning run,
to step outside and watch your breath freeze
into clouds in front of your face while you jog
in place, waiting for your watch to synch.
It's a lot to remember to put the trash bins out
each Thursday night, to pull them back in Friday
morning, empty and ready to accept all we throw away.
It's a lot to do the daily exercises your physical
therapist has prescribed, to know it's good
for your body but to still begrudge them anyway.
To hike with your dog every single day, to know
one skipped day, because of crappy weather
or a meeting that runs long or just because
you're tired, is a day she'll be more anxious—
it's a lot. And to try to love openly, to be quick
with forgiveness and slow with frustration.
It's a lot to not eat a dozen chocolate chip
cookies as you pull them warm from the oven.
It's a lot to floss each day, to wear a mask anytime
you venture out, and to not scream at your friends
who post pictures clearly violating the six-foot rule.
And to work your way down your to-do list knowing
you'll add two things for every one you cross off,
it's a lot. It's a lot get a call from your brother
and then one from your sister, for them to relay
the doctors' messages. And it's a lot to know
the only time you flew this year was not to taste
a new country or to get lost on the cramped streets
of a foreign land, but to say goodbye. To hold
your father's hand and kiss his cheek—it's a lot
to know it was for the last time. It's a lot to meal
plan and grocery shop and not be annoyed
when there are no snacks in the house when you
purposefully did not buy snacks. And it's a lot
to support your friend through chemo,

and your other friend through her son's diagnosis,
to swim through your own grief. And to put
on pants every day and write poems and emails
and calendar reminders, it's a lot. And this life,
this beautiful, wretched, complicated, glorious life.
It's a lot.

II.

Do not be afraid that joy will make pain worse;
it is needed like the air we breathe.
~ Göran Persson

A Quatern About Joy

I'm trying to write about joy
but instead think of his hands,
his mouth against my wrist,
my heartbeat pounding against his lips.

I want to talk about the sunsets we watched but
I'm trying to write about joy
and every time the ocean swallowed the sun
I knew it was another day gone.

I think of the salt air that licked skin,
his hands tangled in my hair,
the joy I'm trying to write about:
my name in his mouth,

Good morning, beautiful, falling from
his lips before he even opened his eyes.
How he always wanted me
to write about joy. I'm trying.

LIKE THAT

~after Kim Addonizio

Love me like a horror film, when the virgin
is stumbling through the dark in a short skirt
and kitten heels—completely impractical yet
anticipated. Love me like the water cascading
from a waterfall, unable to stop its headlong
dive over the rocky edge. Do it without asking—
swipe the salt-shaker from the diner, walk out
on the check. Love me like a hurricane,
meteorologists predicting a path you refuse
to follow. Tear up the coast and head inland,
toss the palm trees like confetti at midnight.
Revel in the mess left in your wake. Do it
in the only bathroom at a house party,
when there's a line queued up and waiting
but I'm balanced on the edge of the sink
and you're between my legs. Wrap your
fist in my hair and pull me close. Watch
in the mirror. Love me when it's late
and the road stretches before us like taffy.
When you're asleep in the passenger
seat and the dog is asleep in the backseat
and only the radio keeps me company.
We'll switch and you'll drive the last three
hours and I'll fight sleep but eventually nod
off and when I wake we'll be home and we'll be
happy there, if you love me like that.

POEM ENDING WITH A NESTLING CRADLED IN MY HUSBAND'S LARGE HAND

Because of the time difference I wake
to a text from my husband, sent the night
before. Perched on the edge of his hand
is a tiny bird, a nestling—already feathered
but not yet able to maintain flight.
The dogs went nuts, he said, *I think it flew
into the front door.* I imagine my dogs,
100 pounds of fur and teeth, unaware
of their strength, beholden to their prey
drive. *I felt like a Disney princess*, he said,
it just sat in my hand, fluttering its wings.
He carried it to a tree at the edge of our
property, gentled it onto a branch, the dogs'
barking escalating to a frenzied pitch. The next
morning another text awaits me: *it didn't
make it.* Instead of imagining it broken
between my dogs' strong jaws, I think
of it in my husband's hand, its small body
protected, its feathered frame safe.

WOULD YOU EVER GET YOUR SPOUSE'S NAME TATTOOED?

~ a question posted on Twitter

We'd been separated six months and you'd been dating
someone for two months when you called to tell me
my name now graced your bicep. I looked at the kitchen
that was now only mine: the fridge with the broken
handle, the stove with only three working burners. *We're not
getting back together*, I finally said. *It's a testament*, you corrected,
to the years we spent together. I was wife #2 and you tell me
your first wife's name was inked onto your other bicep.
But where will you put your third wife's name? I quipped. *I'll never
marry again*, you insisted. Years later I will spend hours
getting my entire left arm tattooed, a delicate sleeve
that my second husband does not like—he cannot
comprehend how they make me feel beautiful. I waited
seven years to remarry, uncertain I wanted to do it again,
uncertain I could. You remarried seven months after
our divorce was finalized. I don't know where
her name resides.

TRUTHS: AN INCOMPLETE LIST

1. I can't give my heart fully.
2. Except to my dogs. They own it all.
3. It's easy to confuse acceptance for happiness.
4. I miss the dark splash of wine coloring my lips.
5. I've almost completely stopped listening to music.
6. Sometimes I imagine your death.
7. Or more accurately, my life after your death.
8. The bruised leaves of fall are my favorite. Even if they're dying, they're lovely.
9. When I got my first mammogram I wondered at all the fuss—I felt no pain, no discomfort.
10. Monica Lewinsky did nothing wrong.
11. My sister does taxidermy. I've grown fearful of opening packages from her.
12. I miss the sun on my skin, his hands in my hair.
13. In my defense, I needed to feel beautiful.
14. Call it a decade of deciding to stay.

ARE ALL THE LOVERS IN YOUR POEMS REAL?

~ after Shannon Wolf, after Aimee Nezhukumatathil

If by real you mean real as a cool
breeze kissing your skin and raising
goosebumps along your arms, then yes,
every touch, every tender word, every
glance is real. Wait. They're not exactly
real because they don't exist in real
time but instead are held in separate
chambers in my heart because I love
them all simultaneously—each lover
a part of me. One saying, *good morning
beautiful*, while another hands me a cup
of coffee and another washes the dishes
from last night's dinner party. Can you
imagine how many bouquets
of ranunculus I'd receive each January?
Each aware of my favorite flower, each
wanting my birthday smile bestowed
upon them, and every single one
of them wonders who I love best.

CRUSH

The first girl I crushed on looked
like a 90s Winona Ryder, all angles
and a pixie haircut. We were the
intersection of a Venn diagram,
the only overlap in our circle
of friends. We didn't hang out
on Friday nights, didn't look
for one another in the crowded
lunchroom—a square of greasy pizza
and an oversized chocolate chip cookie
on our lunch trays. We had few things
in common—me in French club and she
in theater, yet still we gravitated toward
one another, touching hands softly
in the crowded hallway in between
classes, those seconds sometimes
the best in my day. Once we walked
to her car after class, a cigarette passed
between us like a secret. I didn't
smoke but it was the closest our mouths
would ever get to touching.

SNAILS & STARS

Snails can sleep for up to three months
which I think just makes them depressed.
But we aren't always good about acknowledging
depression in people so are we capable
of recognizing it in other creatures? I doubt it.

My best friend has suffered from severe
depression for more than twenty years.
She tells me she can't imagine living
another forty years feeling like this. *I don't want
to die*, she says, *I just want to go to sleep
forever.*

I tell her about the snail and suggest
she'll be one in her next life. Her psychiatrist
changes her meds, her therapist suggests
magnet therapy, I pour her another glass,
the bubbles streaking by like shooting stars.

Last year, a friend took a bottle of pills and went
to sleep. At his memorial we watched
the slideshow, his smiling face in every frame,
the galaxy of his friends spilling onto the lawn.
We are a constellation of caring, but we were not
enough to save him.

My best friend and I sit on the couch,
two dogs curled between us, content
as snails in their shells. I've known her
for over half my life. I want her
for double that.

CROOKED

I have an extra vertebra, 25 to the normal
24, but I don't think this makes me special.
The opposite is true: I am freak, strange,
mutant. While in the locker room
I see a young girl unclasp the rigid brace
that holds her straight. I try not to stare.
How I wish I'd had one, how I wish my
parents, the doctors, the school had caught
the sideways shuffle my spine started dancing.
What the world would be like if I didn't tilt a little,
if the curve of my body was just a feminine
silhouette rather than chronic pain, if the x-rays
didn't require a protractor to measure
the bend—the only time I've ever used
geometry. The massage therapist notices:
how one side is higher than the other, how
my hip pulls up on one side, how my shoulder
tugs down to try to meet it. The physical
therapist notices, teaches me exercises to try
to balance the forever-unbalanced. And
at night I lie in bed, stretch my crooked
body long before settling in. I can feel
my spine pressing into the bed, perfect
pressure applied. I fall asleep feeling
weightless, tired and tangled, my body
curving in toward my heart.

IF THERE IS A GOD

She's pissed. Hair-pulling, spit-flying,
curse-screaming pissed. She looks
down on her creation and wonders
where she went wrong. She gave us
everything—art and science, rainforests
and medicine, grasslands and goats,
narwhals and math and poetry.
And we continue to fuck it up.
She thinks about the rapture, something
she never considered or promised,
thinks, *maybe I should…* But then
COVID appears and she decides to wait.
When doctors and scientists create
the vaccine she exclaims, *Praise me!*
They are not a lost cause! But then she sees
the antivaxxers, the ones who won't
wear masks, she hears the protests
of *my body, my choice* and rolls her eyes
because women—the beings
she created after her own image—
have so little autonomy in the world
she made in six days. She contemplates
wiping everything away and starting
again—another flood perhaps?
Instead, she changes into her pajamas,
the buttery soft material gliding across
her perfect skin. She crawls into bed
and turns out the light. Prays
to herself that tomorrow will be better.

How to Run

Lace up your shoes, put one foot
in front of the other. Repeat until
his name is no longer circling
in your mind, until all you hear
and think and breathe is your footfall,
gentle against the pavement.
Invest in good shoes, sweat-wicking
clothes and a quality sports bra: trust
me, it's worth the cost. When it's raining,
wear a visor to keep your vision clear—
you'll still need to log your miles. If you
don't, you'll curl up on the couch, phone
in your hand, scrolling through pictures
of him. You'll want to call him so run
an extra mile instead, run until you're soaked
through, shoes sloshing with every
step, but you're no longer tempted
to hear his voice. Wake with the sunrise,
watch the sky lighten as you crest
a hill, your gait easier than it's been
in weeks. Run faster, push your pace
until your legs quake and every atom
aches from something that isn't his touch.
Sleep hard every night, your body wonderfully
exhausted. Dream of the hills you will tackle
the next morning. Wake rested and ready,
your body craving movement, your mind
clear and unencumbered by any thoughts
other than today's route. Lace up your shoes,
put one foot in front of the other. Repeat.

DISCOVERY

Let me rename this anxiety a discovery,
let me call it the late-blooming flower,
the lilacs that popped purple on my
neighbor's bush the last week
in October. Maybe that flower knew
I needed it, knew I'd spent seven
weeks locked in a brace that spooned
my body in a thigh-to-ankle embrace,
the crutches confining me to one room.
But on that first walk with my dogs around
the block I spotted the out-of-season
blooms, the pale purple clusters hanging
heavy against a backdrop of leaves
already turning yellow and gold.
I could blame climate change, could
proclaim this a sign of nature losing
its mind, the seasons no longer
staying true and dictating when
things grow or hibernate or bloom.
Instead I'll assume those flowers
knew I needed their heavy scent,
their gentle color, their small petals
to brush against my skin as I buried
my nose and inhaled.

PROMPTS

Write a poem about the person who got away. Write in red pen, let the ink represent the blood pounding through your heart. Detail the backs of their hands, how they felt against your skin, how your body burned for them. Burn the poem. Watch the flames consume the paper. Inhale the smoke as you stand ready with the extinguisher—do not let it consume anything else, it has eaten enough of your heart.

Write a poem about the sunrise. Do not use the word *palette* or *watercolor* or *sky* or *morning*. Describe the impenetrable black before the pledge of color. Write about your thoughts in those moments of darkness, how your heart battles with your brain to decide if this version of life is enough. Reassure the reader that by the time the murky promise of day has been realized in the stinging bright sunshine that you are okay—you don't want every poem to crush your reader.

Write a poem in the form of a diary entry. Confess your secrets—the man you kissed after too much wine, how he pushed you against the brick of the building and you wanted those stones permanently tattooed onto your back. List each place you fucked him—the beach, the backseat, the bathroom of the crowded party. Leave this poem on a bench at the bus stop, let a stranger read it and know your secret now runs free.

Write a poem asking forgiveness—for the lies you told, for the trespasses you committed, for your fickle heart. List them one to one hundred, use permanent marker, write in ALL CAPS. When this list is complete, bake it inside a loaf of bread, your mother's recipe. Cut a piece while it's still warm, feel the heat scorch your fingertips. Watch the butter melt, the bread turning golden. With each bite you swallow, forgive yourself.

III.

Happy

My husband says I need to talk
to someone who isn't him or the dogs
and so every week I drop bombshells
on my therapist: my mom's a bitch,
I hate my job, I'm scared
to travel, my sister-in-law's son died
and no one knows why, I'm counting
calories again, my dad is dying, my dad
is dead.

And then once everything I am scared
of happening happened and that
bucket of anxiety and fear and worry
and doubt I am holding with shaking
arms gets dumped out then the next day
it rains and everything is washed away
and I take my dogs on a hike and the trails
are a muddy mess and I slip down a small
hill and my butt and the dogs are all
a muddy mess but the sky is sapphire
and the sun is warm and the trails
are empty and the streams are full
of clear water and the dogs and I drink
our fill and I talk to my dad which
is basically just talking to myself but
a butterfly wings by and one dog snaps
her jaws at it and I laugh and am covered
in mud and I am happy.

Shopping for a Dress for My Father's Funeral

I prefer consignment shops, don't like
paying full price. My father, the ultimate
bargain shopper, would be proud.
After retiring he became a regular
at yard and estate sales, graduating
to auctions where they sold unpaid
storage units. My dad spent hours
combing through them, searching
for what he deemed valuable or worth
salvaging. He furnished my first
apartment this way, showing up
unannounced with a couch and a table
and a bed. I think my father would
appreciate this show of thriftiness, my desire
for a deal. I flip through the racks now,
discard most, nothing is right
for a funeral. I try on a few, sit
in the dressing room and cry. Leave
without buying any.

WE OPEN CARDS AFTER MY FATHER'S MEMORIAL SERVICE

and inside I find cash. I lift the twenty into the air.
What the hell? My mother assures me it's normal,
a small way for loved ones to offset the cost
of death. It seems so macabre—birthday cards
are supposed to contain cash, not cards decorated
with soft sayings and muted flowers. The ones that
contain a note informing us a donation has been
made to the church my father hasn't attended
in forty years annoy me the most—we specified
two places: the hospice that helped ease him
into the end and the foundation that fights
the disease that led him there—this is where we
wanted the money to go. After all the cards
have been opened and read my mother counts
the cash: $175. That night we get pizza,
my father pays the bill.

I Watched Jaws as a Kid and Have Been Afraid of Sharks Ever Since

I wake at midnight, sharks
of anxiety circling me in the water.
This bed is no life raft but I cling
to it anyway, hoping it saves me.
At 1am my dog's nails click
softly against the hardwood
and I realize the ocean around me
has receded. My other dog wakes, fearful
of being left out, and I take them both
for a walk. It's raining, a quiet sluice
of water falling around us. They spot
a tiny mouse scurrying along the wet
pavement and it screams before I can
pull them back, 100 pounds of fur and teeth
descending on the small creature. Back
inside I towel them off, climb the stairs
to bed, the water chasing me up every step.
My husband slumbers beside me, safe
in his dreams. The shrill screaming loops
in my mind and I cling to the comforter,
hoping it'll save me. When I finally fall
asleep the rain has diminished to a quiet
mist. The sharks still circle, even in sleep
they keep moving, my anxiety flowing over
their gills, keeping them alive.

AFTER CRYING ABOUT MY DAD, I MASTURBATE

Because if I don't I might
dream of him and I can't
face that again. The last time
I woke with tears leaking out
of eyes still crusty from sleep
and my whole day was blue
with memories. So tonight, after
crying because I'll never again
hear my father's voice, I grab
my phone and read erotica.
It distracts me enough that
my hand moves south
and I close my eyes, focus
my energy. Eventually I fall
asleep, hand on my belly, fingertips
caught in the elastic of my underwear.
I dream only of the ocean, huge
waves crashing over my boat, the salty
water running down my face like tears.

THE USUAL THINGS

Quinn says we can pick the thing we fear, choose
our anxiety. Our brains are going to focus on something
so we may as well choose which direction it goes. I think
of the 8-foot tall animatronic clown that stands by the gas
station closest to my house. Its white skin and red hair,
the sharpened teeth and the way its arms and head move
jerkily from side-to-side. I stare at it as I wait for the light
to change, always look away when its head swivels in my
direction. I've never seen the movie, the previews alone
were enough to make me tug my dog's leash when she moves
too close to the storm drain—I know this is where evil lurks,
even in my nice neighborhood. And the Exorcist stairs,
the ones the priest was thrown down, those are less than
five miles from my house. I've run up them, there are 75 steps
and they're steep. It's another movie I haven't watched,
that scene where the little girl spiderwalks down the stairs
backwards is enough to give me nightmares for weeks.
But maybe now is the time to watch them, to give myself
something other-worldly to fear. Because it's the eve
of the election and a close friend has a brain tumor
and it's been two months since my dad died. All of these
things crowd my brain and fight for attention, the anxiety
and fear climbing each day. So maybe I should watch
the scary movies: that evil clown with the razor teeth,
the girl with the spinning head, the boogeyman in the closet.
Everything will still be there when we turn the lights on, after
the popcorn is eaten, and the credits roll. But maybe that night
I'll worry only about the storm drain, I'll check under the bed
and behind the curtains, I'll go to bed haunted, but not
by the usual things.

WHAT THIS ELEGY WANTS

~ after Tarfia Faizullah

It doesn't want flowers
or flowery language,

in fact, it wants to quiet
the poet in me. It wants

to remind me my father
was of the earth and wants

wheat instead of white lilies,
wants soybeans and sunflowers

and the seeds he spread each
spring. After he quit

farming he planted a garden
and every summer we bonded

over tomatoes and cucumbers,
the mint I had to tear

up at the root to stop it
from taking over. And when

he died in the fall my garden
kept producing, as if he was there,

gentling the vegetables into giving
more. Each time I buried

my hands in the soil I talked
to my father, certain he could

hear me, certain his hands
were covering mine, guiding

me as I weeded and thinned
and harvested. What this elegy

wants is a garden every summer,
the sun kissing the seedlings

that burst through the ground, my
hands digging quietly. This elegy

wants earth and sunshine and soft
rain. This elegy wants my hands

in the dirt, my father in the soil
of my heart, growing long past

the season of his life.

BREATH

When they tell you to stop talking about death
in your poems talk about breath instead, how

your father's slowed, a shallow gulp every
20 or 30 seconds, so spaced out you started

holding your own breath in response, as if the rise
and fall of your chest would drag your father's with it.

Think about how you breathe when you run,
as the miles stretch out before you and your legs settle

into a steady pace, the rhythm your breath mimics.
Remember the legend about your father racing

his friends at the dirt track. How he took off
his shoes and ran barefoot and kicked all their asses.

Dream of Jason, whose lungs filled with fluid
from birth, how each breath was a battle.

How the pink lungs he was gifted only bought
him another two weeks. Two weeks of tubes and clean

rooms and clutching his hand through latex gloves.
Think of the breath-work you learned in yoga,

the ujjayi pranayama practice meant to mimic ocean
waves. Think of the days you spent with him on the beach,

the sand between your toes, the salt coating your skin
and curling your hair. How every time you watched

the ocean swallow the sun it was a small death—
of that day, of your time together, of your heart.

Remember the last night, how you found your mother
asleep in the living room, your father silent on the bed

by the window. How his breath was the only sound
as the sun rose. Remember how it was quiet, the rattle

had faded, replaced by tiny sips of air until even this
stopped. And then the only sound was the gulp

of your wail.

BLOOD CLAIM

My sister claims my dad's overalls, cinches
the suspenders until they fit. He wore them
when the temperatures dropped, when he
walked the dog in the frigid mornings,
the frosted grass crunching under their feet.

I claim my grandmother's green depression
glass bowls. For years they sat on a shelf
in my parents' house, unused.

My sister is learning to hunt, raises the gun
to her shoulder and exhales slowly, her body
still and warm, the air clouding in front of her
mouth. She'll darken the knees with the blood
of an animal, a dark red-brown stain that never
completely washes out.

I wash the bowl by hand, finger the grooves
cut into the glass. That night I fill it with
leeks and beets, the kale I've massaged
with lemon. The beets bleed purple
onto the glass. It rinses clean
in the soapy water.

While Trying to Write a Poem I Realize I Have Nothing to Write About So I Contemplate Having an Affair

Because that would at least give me something
to write about. But I think of all the reasons I shouldn't:
I'd have to wear something other than yoga pants,
have to go somewhere other than the grocery store
or the park because, despite romantic comedies, I'm not
meeting anyone there. I'd probably need to not wear
a mask and with that realization my plan goes out
the window because no way in hell am I going
maskless around someone I don't know. And no,
I didn't include "because I'm married" to the list
because that's a requirement for an affair. But this
idea fails, just as this poem is failing, so I saddle up
this sad pony and ride right off the page to the poem
graveyard, which is littered with bones of cliches
and repeated words (mouth, hands, touch, taste),
the discarded bodies of the lovers I've written
about endlessly, the images I can't stop repeating,
the ocean in my throat that keeps drowning the words,
the death that haunts every line. When I get there
I settle onto the soft earth, dig my fingers into
the freshly turned soil and think of my father,
how he once saddled a cow and donned a wig
and rode it in a parade, and how this remains
one of my favorite stories about him, how it made
the front page of the local paper, how my mother still
has a copy. And I think of how, under that hot July
sun, I held him in my hand, opened my palm,
and the wind tornadoed him back to the land
he loved. To the land that grazed cattle and grew
crops and I decide maybe I do have something
to write about.

BLESSING FOR THE GIRLS WITH EATING DISORDERS

Because I know what it's like to make lists of food
you'll never allow yourself to eat, to let your fingers
trip through a cookbook, using Post-Its to mark
recipes you'll never make. Bless the girls who see
a buffet as the most deliciously terrifying thing,
whose friends marvel at her getting seconds
and thirds, without knowing she'll kneel before
the toilet and, without a sound, bring everything
back up—the eating reversed until the very first
thing she swallowed brushes past her teeth and
kisses her lips as it leaves. Bless the girls who log
every morsel they eat, who know the calorie
count of every meal, who track their workouts
and calories and go to sleep with the dull ache
of hunger in their bellies. Bless the ones who break
the cycle and the ones who don't. Bless the girls
who see themselves in this poem. Bless the girl
writing it, for the words reflecting in her eyes
and feeling like home.

ODE TO OCTOPUS

Because you can squeeze into (and out of) small
spaces, you've never worried about your size.
You happily devour fish and mussels and crabs,
food held in your many arms, never afraid
you are too much. Your hearts pump blue blood
to each appendage as you reach into rocks
and coral, pulling the white flesh from a conch
shell, searching for your next snack. Oh, how I long
to be that carefree, to hold bread in one hand
and chocolate in the other. To fill my belly
and fulfill my desires without thinking of the scale
tucked into the corner. You, with suckers
lining your arms like bangles, are not afraid
to take up space, to hold onto what you want.
How I wish to emulate you, to stake my claim
at the buffet, to not think twice about wanting.

EVERY LAST BITE

Last summer, I thumbed through
old photos while my father's breathing
chainsawed from the corner. Until
the braces came off—three years
of bands and headgear, my jaw expanded,
the shark row of teeth reduced
and realigned to the white picket
fence in my mouth—I didn't smile,
every photo a tight-lipped exposition.
My parents' wedding photo watches
my father reach for breath. He too
was tight-lipped. After the wedding
my mother took him to the dentist,
his first in his 24 years. They excavated
his mouth, pulled the rot from his skull,
and handed him porcelain to anchor
his smile. When I got braces it was
my father who drove me an hour each
way, his dedication to my mouth
a desire to not grow into him. As he lies
dying we leave his dentures in, even
though he can no longer chew or even
swallow, the morphine absorbed
through the soft flesh of his cheek.
Before they reduce his body to ash,
they remove the placeholder in his
mouth. His smile watches as the flames
catch, consuming every last bite of him.

THE PLAINS SPEAK GRIEF

It's easy to get lost here—with nothing
but wide open a person can wander
for weeks without finding shelter.
Men have plowed and planted, hoed
and harvested, been nurtured
and broken by this land—it's not always
my fault but if a farmer doesn't learn
grief early he'll never make it. But
the other side of grief is love and I've
got that in spades too. I'll bless that
4am wake-up with a fuchsia sunrise.
I'll give that late night chore a blanket
of stars pulled tight across the sky.
And long after that farmer has sold
his tractor and held the last shafts
of wheat between his fingers, I'll give
him a soft breeze against his sun-darkened
skin. I'll stretch cerulean like a quilt
across a summer sky. And during
the last week of his life, when
his daughter can't sleep and he's
clutching at breath from the hospital
bed, I'll give her the most brilliant
sunrise she's ever seen. I'll paint the sky
magenta and violet, I'll show her
the brutal beauty of grief, I'll let her tears
water the thistle that grows wild
in the ditches, and she'll know I'll hold
him in the earth of my hands and he'll
be home.

FATHER, LET ME

Father, digger of dirt, planter
of seeds—1,000 acres of wide open
and four babies by 33. Fingernails black
with soil and blood, calves birthed
in the early spring hours, babies born
at hours he no longer remembers.
Father, brown-skinned and steel-toed
boots, coveralls, and a new tractor. Black
hair and creased skin, a permanent
squint against the bright. Father
in fields to watch the sunrise
and sunset, the hills hypnotizing
as the combine cuts the wheat, a steady
pattern under your hands. Father, bones
exhausted, body spent. Father lay
quiet, let me clean the blood
from under your nails, let me wipe
the dirt from your face, let me
be something you're proud of.

ACKNOWLEDGEMENTS & NOTES

The poet kindly thanks the following journals which first gave her poems a home, sometimes in earlier forms:

Ample Remains: "Crush," "Every Last Bite"

Bitchin' Kitsch: "We Open Cards After My Father's Memorial Service"

Bending Genres: "While Trying to Write a Poem I Realize I Have Nothing to Write About So I Contemplate Having an Affair"

Bourgeon: "Poem Ending With a Nestling Cradled in My Husband's Large Hand," "Would You Ever Get Your Spouse's Name Tattooed?," "Blessing for the Girls With Eating Disorders"

Brave Voices Magazine: "When My Therapist Asks How I'm Doing," "Crooked"

The Broadkill Review: "Snails & Stars"

Call Me [Brackets]: "Self-Portrait"

Dead Skunk: "Blood Claim"

Dodging the Rain: "It's a Lot"

Ethel Zine: "After Crying About My Dad, I Masturbate"

FEED Magazine: "I Watched Jaws as a Kid and Have Been Afraid of Sharks Ever Since"

Heavy Feather Review: "We Feed the Living"

Heimat Review: "The Plains Speak Grief"

The Hellebore: "Shopping for a Dress for My Father's Funeral"

Identity Theory: "I Don't Understand Black Holes No Matter How Many Times Cody Explains Them to Me"

Levitate Magazine: "The Usual Things"

Limp Wrist: "Small," "If There is a God"

Mausoleum Press: "Truths: An Incomplete List"

Neoligism Poetry Journal: "A Quatern About Joy"

perhappened: "How to Run"

Pine Hills Review: "You Ain't Shit"

Punk Noir Magazine: "Tender Muscle"

Quail Bell Magazine: "Happy," "What This Elegy Wants"

River Mouth Review: "I Don't Eat After 8pm"

Screen Door Review: "Menagerie"

Snapdragon Journal: "Discovery"

vulnery magazine: "Like That"

Welter: "Father, Let Me"

Whale Road Review: "The Night My Father Died We Made My Brother-in-Law Watch Dirty Dancing"

YAWP: "Breath"

"For My Friends, in Response to a Question" was inspired by *"For My Friends, in Reply to a Question"* by Safia Elhillo

"It's a Lot" was inspired by a poem with the same title by Jon Sands

"Like That" was inspired by a poem with the same title by Kim Addonizio

"Are All the Lovers in Your Poems Real?" was inspired by the poem *"Are All the Fathers in Your Poems Real?"* by Shannon Wolf, which was inspired by the poem *"Are All the Break-Ups in Your Poems Real?"* by Aimee Nezhukumatathil

"What This Elegy Wants" was inspired by a poem with the same title by Tarfia Faizullah

THANKS

Thanks to Derrick Brown and Nikki Steele at Write Bloody for your guidance and energy. I'm grateful to be a part of the WB family. Thank you to my editor, Anna Binkovitz, for her feedback and brilliance.

Thanks to Melissa Fite Johnson, Laura Passin, Megan Falley, Shuly Cawood, and Barbara Costas-Biggs for the beautiful blurbs.

Thanks to my writing group: Ashley Steineger, Chelsea Risley, Caroline Earleywine, Barbara Costas-Biggs, and Amy Haddad—you've read and provided feedback on each of these poems and they're stronger because of it. Special thanks to Ashley who beta read this manuscript in an earlier form.

Thank you to Seema Reza and Community Building Art Works, and to Jon Sands and the Emotional Historians—so many of these poems were birthed in your workshops. Thank you for the inspiration and space.

Thanks to my sister, Kirsten Birst, for her never-ending support and to my best friend, Virginia Willett—the world is better with you in it, thank you every day for deciding to stay. Thank you to Heather Sullivan for always being ready with a shovel.

Thanks to Sita Romero and Whitney Hill for every motherfucking pep talk.

Thanks to Piper and Cricket—yes, I know, dogs can't read, but these pups save me time and again and own my heart.

Thanks to my husband, Jay, for his support and love.

Thank you to the readers who see themselves in these poems. I'm holding space for you.

ABOUT THE AUTHOR

COURTNEY LEBLANC is the author of the full-length collections Her Whole Bright Life (winner of the Jack McCarthy Book Prize, Write Bloody, 2023); Exquisite Bloody, Beating Heart (Riot in Your Throat, 2021); and Beautiful & Full of Monsters (Vegetarian Alcoholic Press, 2020). She is a Virginia Center for Creative Arts fellow (2022) and the founder and editor-in-chief of Riot in Your Throat, an independent poetry press. She loves nail polish, tattoos, and a soy latte each morning. Find her online at www.CourtneyLeBlanc.com. Follow her on Twitter: @wordperv, and Instagram: @wordperv79.

If You Like Courtney LeBlanc, Courtney Likes...

Racing Hummingbirds
Jeanann Verlee

Said the Manic to the Muse
Jeanann Verlee

After the Witch Hunt
Megan Falley

Redhead and the Slaughter King

Megan Falley

A Constellation of Half-Lives
Seema Reza

Write Bloody Publishing publishes and promotes great books of poetry every year.
We believe that poetry can change the world for the better. We are an independent press
dedicated to quality literature and book design, with an office
in Los Angeles, California.

We are grassroots, DIY, bootstrap believers. Pull up a good book and join the family.
Support independent authors, artists, and presses.

Want to know more about Write Bloody books, authors, and events?
Join our mailing list at

www.writebloody.com

WRITE BLOODY BOOKS

After the Witch Hunt — Megan Falley

Aim for the Head: An Anthology of Zombie Poetry — Rob Sturma, Editor

Allow The Light: The Lost Poems of Jack McCarthy — Jessica Lohafer, Editor

Amulet — Jason Bayani

Any Psalm You Want — Khary Jackson

Atrophy — Jackson Burgess

Birthday Girl with Possum — Brendan Constantine

The Bones Below — Sierra DeMulder

Born in the Year of the Butterfly Knife — Derrick C. Brown

Bouquet of Red Flags — Taylor Mali

Bring Down the Chandeliers — Tara Hardy

Ceremony for the Choking Ghost — Karen Finneyfrock

A Constellation of Half-Lives — Seema Reza

Counting Descent — Clint Smith

Courage: Daring Poems for Gutsy Girls — Karen Finneyfrock,
Mindy Nettifee, & Rachel McKibbens, Editors

Cut to Bloom — Arhm Choi Wild

Dear Future Boyfriend — Cristin O'Keefe Aptowicz

Do Not Bring Him Water — Caitlin Scarano

Don't Smell the Floss — Matty Byloos

Drive Here and Devastate Me — Megan Falley

Drunks and Other Poems of Recovery — Jack McCarthy

The Elephant Engine High Dive Revival — Derrick C. Brown, Editor

Every Little Vanishing — Sheleen McElhinney

Everyone I Love Is a Stranger to Someone — Annelyse Gelman

Everything Is Everything — Cristin O'Keefe Aptowicz

Favorite Daughter — Nancy Huang

The Feather Room — Anis Mojgani

Floating, Brilliant, Gone — Franny Choi

Glitter in the Blood: A Poet's Manifesto for Better, Braver Writing — Mindy Nettifee

Gold That Frames the Mirror — Brandon Melendez

The Heart of a Comet — Pages D. Matam

Heavy Lead Birdsong — Ryler Dustin

Hello. It Doesn't Matter. — Derrick C. Brown

Help in the Dark Season — Jacqueline Suskin

Hot Teen Slut — Cristin O'Keefe Aptowicz

How the Body Works the Dark — Derrick C. Brown

How to Love the Empty Air — Cristin O'Keefe Aptowicz

I Love Science! — Shanny Jean Maney

I Love You Is Back — Derrick C. Brown

The Importance of Being Ernest — Ernest Cline

The Incredible Sestina Anthology — Daniel Nester, Editor

In Search of Midnight — Mike McGee

In the Pockets of Small Gods — Anis Mojgani

Junkyard Ghost Revival — Derrick C. Brown, Editor

Kissing Oscar Wilde — Jade Sylvan

The Last American Valentine — Derrick C. Brown, Editor

The Last Time as We Are — Taylor Mali

Learn Then Burn — Tim Stafford & Derrick C. Brown, Editors

Learn Then Burn Teacher's Guide — Tim Stafford & Molly Meacham, Editors

Learn Then Burn 2: This Time It's Personal — Tim Stafford, Editor

Lessons on Being Tenderheaded — Janae Johnson

Love in a Time of Robot Apocalypse — David Perez

The Madness Vase — Andrea Gibson

Multiverse: An Anthology of Superhero Poetry of Superhuman Proportions —
Rob Sturma & Ryk McIntyre, Editors

My, My, My, My, My — Tara Hardy

The New Clean — Jon Sands

New Shoes on a Dead Horse — Sierra DeMulder

No Matter the Wreckage — Sarah Kay

Oh God Get Out Get Out — Bill Moran

Oh, Terrible Youth — Cristin O'Keefe Aptowicz

1,000 Black Umbrellas — Daniel McGinn

Time Bomb Snooze Alarm — Bucky Sinister

Uh-Oh — Derrick C. Brown

Uncontrolled Experiments in Freedom — Brian S. Ellis

The Undisputed Greatest Writer of All Time — Beau Sia

The Way We Move Through Water — Lino Anunciacion

We Will Be Shelter — Andrea Gibson, Editor

What Learning Leaves — Taylor Mali

What the Night Demands — Miles Walser

Working Class Represent — Cristin O'Keefe Aptowicz

Workin' Mime to Five — Dick Richards

Write About an Empty Birdcage — Elaina Ellis

Yarmulkes & Fitted Caps — Aaron Levy Samuels

The Year of No Mistakes — Cristin O'Keefe Aptowicz

Yesterday Won't Goodbye — Brian S. Ellis

CPSIA information can be obtained
at www.ICGtesting.com
Printed in the USA
JSHW020226210423
40616JS00003B/162